Children's Authors

Cynthia Rylant

Jill C. Wheeler
ABDO Publishing Company

visit us at
www.abdopublishing.com

Published by ABDO Publishing Company, 8000 West 78th Street, Edina, Minnesota 55439. Copyright © 2009 by Abdo Consulting Group, Inc. International copyrights reserved in all countries. No part of this book may be reproduced in any form without written permission from the publisher. The Checkerboard Library™ is a trademark and logo of ABDO Publishing Company.

Printed in the United States.

Photo credits: Alamy p. 13; AP Images pp. 9, 11; Corbis pp. 7, 15; Doug Oudekerk p. 5; Simon & Schuster p. 19

Editors: Tamara L. Britton, Megan M. Gunderson
Art Direction: Neil Klinepier

Library of Congress Cataloging-in-Publication Data

Wheeler, Jill C., 1964-
  Cynthia Rylant / Jill C. Wheeler.
       p. cm. -- (Children's authors)
  Includes bibliographical references and index.
  ISBN 978-1-60453-079-7
 1. Rylant, Cynthia--Juvenile literature. 2. Authors, American--20th century--Biography--Juvenile literature. I. Title.

 PS3568.Y55Z95 2009
 813'.54--dc22
 [B]
                                        2008004803

Contents

Drawing on Real Life

Cynthia Rylant has written more than 80 books. These include the award-winning *When I Was Young in the Mountains*, *Missing May*, and *A Fine White Dust*. Rylant has written fiction, nonfiction, and poetry. She has also written **autobiographies** and illustrated picture books.

Rylant is a very private person. In fact, the name Cynthia Rylant is a **pseudonym**. Yet her fans can learn a lot about her by reading her books. Much of Rylant's fiction draws on her childhood experiences in rural West Virginia.

Some of Rylant's nonfiction also comes from real life. In her autobiography *But I'll Be Back Again,* Rylant details her childhood and teenage years. In *Best Wishes*, she writes about her adult life. She also discusses writing as well as returning to visit West Virginia.

Rylant credits much of her creativity to the challenges she faced as a child. Losing her father is one reason she turned to writing. Writing books has helped Rylant better understand her own experiences.

Cynthia Rylant

Childhood Challenge

Cynthia Rylant was born Cynthia Smith on June 6, 1954, in Hopewell, Virginia. Her father, John Smith, was a sergeant in the U.S. Army. He fought in the **Korean War**. Her mother, Leatrel Smith, would become a nurse.

For the first years of her life, Cynthia lived in Illinois. She remembers little about that time, except that her parents fought a lot. Her father drank too much alcohol. He had also caught **hepatitis** during the war. Over time, the alcohol and the disease caused his health to fail.

When Cynthia was four years old, she and her mother moved to Cool Ridge, West Virginia. There, they lived with Leatrel's parents. Several months later, Leatrel left to attend nursing school. Cynthia stayed behind with her grandparents. Cynthia was devastated. She had lost both parents in just a few short months.

John and Leatrel both wrote letters to Cynthia. But soon, John's letters stopped coming. Leatrel continued to write to her daughter. She also visited Cynthia in Cool Ridge several times each year.

Cynthia loved seeing her mother during those short visits. Yet it was very painful each time her mother left. Cynthia would lie on her bed and cry until she had no tears left.

General Ulysses S. Grant made his headquarters in Hopewell during part of the Civil War. This famous picture of him was taken there in 1865.

Young in the Mountains

Cynthia missed her parents. But, she had many other family members in Cool Ridge. In addition to her grandparents, there were aunts, uncles, and cousins to keep her company.

Cynthia and her grandparents lived in a white, four-room home. It had no running water or indoor plumbing. There was a **privy** for the family's use.

Like many other families in Cool Ridge, they had little money. Cynthia's grandfather was a coal miner. But one day, he was hurt in an accident and could no longer work. After that, the family made do as best they could.

When Cynthia was eight years old, her mother finished school. She and her mother moved to their own apartment in the nearby town of Beaver, West Virginia. The apartment had a television, running water, and indoor plumbing. Cynthia was very excited to have an indoor toilet!

Opposite page: *Today, West Virginia's coal miners produce 15 percent of the nation's coal. Coal mining is dangerous work. Miners work with heavy machinery deep underground.*

Early Influences

Cynthia was thrilled to be with her mother again. She also enjoyed living in a larger town. In Beaver, she could spend time with other boys and girls.

In 1964, Cynthia and her girlfriends were swept away by a new musical group. The group was called The Beatles. Cynthia's favorite Beatle was Paul McCartney. She had pictures of him all over her room. Cynthia dreamed of someday meeting him in person.

In addition to listening to music, Cynthia enjoyed reading comic books and Nancy Drew mysteries. Those were about the only books she could get her hands on. She and her mother did not have much extra money to spend on books. And, Beaver had no public library.

During these years, three important events occurred in Cynthia's life. The first was when the New Orleans Symphony Orchestra played at her school. Cynthia loved the music. It made her imagine she was someone else with a different life.

The next was when Robert F. Kennedy stopped in Beaver during his presidential campaign. Cynthia got to shake his hand.

The third event happened when Cynthia was 13 years old. Suddenly, her father began sending her letters again! In them, he talked about getting together with Cynthia sometime.

Cynthia was excited about seeing her father again. Yet before they could meet, he died. Cynthia felt as though she had lost her father twice. She had never been able to get to know him. Perhaps worst of all, she never got to say good-bye.

Robert F. Kennedy was killed on June 5, 1968, just two months after his visit to Beaver.

Bitten by the Book Bug

Cynthia finished her school years like many other teenagers. She enjoyed dating and going to movies with her friends. Cynthia was the head **drum majorette** of the school marching band. She was also president of many school groups.

After high school, Cynthia registered at Morris Harvey College in Charleston, West Virginia. She was planning on a career as a nurse, much like her mother. But after taking her first college English course, Cynthia decided against nursing school.

Cynthia had always loved stories. However, she had never had access to many books. At college, that changed. Cynthia became an enthusiastic reader and fell in love with words. She eventually became the **editor** of the campus newspaper.

Opposite page: *Morris Harvey College is now called the University of Charleston.*

A Brand New World

At college, Rylant did well and earned good grades. She loved school. When she earned her bachelor's **degree** in 1975, she wanted to continue learning. So, Rylant decided to go to **graduate school**.

Rylant began pursuing a master's degree at Marshall University in Huntington, West Virginia. She graduated in 1976. Shortly after that, she married. Her new husband taught classical guitar and was learning to be a carpenter.

Rylant took a job in the children's section of Huntington's public library. She soon found herself reading the books she was supposed to be shelving! The books opened up a whole new world to her.

Here were the books that had not been available to Rylant as a child. She stayed up all night reading them. Soon, she began writing children's books herself.

Rylant continued writing after the birth of her son, Nathaniel. Nathaniel was six months old when Rylant wrote a book about her childhood experiences in Cool Ridge. She finished the entire text of the book within one hour. It is called *When I Was Young in the Mountains*.

Rylant sent the book to a publisher in New York. The publisher accepted it, and it was published in 1982. Diane Goode illustrated the book. It was named a **Caldecott Honor Book** in 1983.

Rylant's childhood in the beautiful Appalachian Mountains inspired her to write **When I Was Young in the Mountains.**

Becoming an Author

Rylant says she's not sure where the words came from for her first book. Yet they seemed to keep on coming! She wrote book after book. Most of the stories were based on things that had happened to her. Sometimes they were exactly like events in her life!

Rylant taught English at Marshall University and the University of Akron.

After a few years of marriage, Rylant and her first husband divorced. Later, she was briefly married to a college professor.

Then, Rylant decided to earn a **degree** in library science. She left West Virginia for Kent, Ohio to attend Kent State University. Rylant earned her **degree** in 1982. Rylant worked as a children's librarian at the Akron Public Library in Akron, Ohio.

Through it all, Rylant kept on writing. In 1984, she published *Waiting to Waltz: A Childhood.* The book is a collection of 30 poems. Like her stories, they capture elements of life in West Virginia.

In 1985, Rylant published her first novel. It is called *A Blue-Eyed Daisy.* The story follows one year in the life of 11-year-old Ellie Farley. Ellie lives in West Virginia. The book offers readers a glimpse into Rylant's own youth and experiences.

Rylant followed her first novel with *The Relatives Came.* The story tells of a family that has relatives visit for the whole summer! Family members sleep on the floor, eat lots of food, and have great fun. Stephen Gammell illustrated the book. It was named a **Caldecott Honor Book** in 1986.

Tackling Tough Topics

Religious faith was an important part of Rylant's childhood in West Virginia. Later, it inspired some of the material in her books. One of Rylant's most well-received books is *A Fine White Dust*. It tells the story of a seventh-grade boy, Pete, who meets a traveling preacher.

The preacher inspires Pete to join the Christian faith. Pete even decides to leave his family and join the preacher in his work. Later, the preacher runs off with a young woman. These events force Pete to examine his faith. They also teach him a lot about what people are like. *A Fine White Dust* was named a **Newbery Honor Book** in 1987.

A Fine White Dust is not the only book in which Rylant has addressed **controversial** topics. She writes about death in her book *Missing May*.

Missing May tells about the loss of a loved one from two different **perspectives**. One is May's 12-year-old niece, Summer. The other is May's husband, Ob. This simple story of

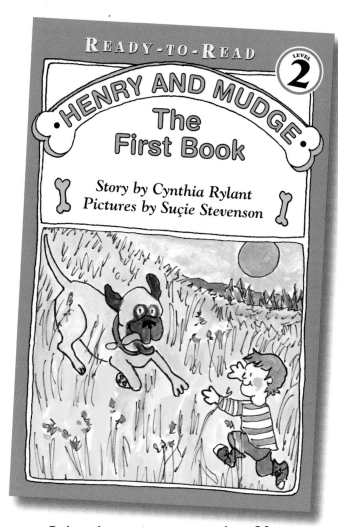

Rylant has written more than 30 stories about Henry and Mudge.

grief and loss touched both children and adults. *Missing May* won the **Newbery Medal** in 1993.

Not all of Rylant's work deals with serious topics. One of her most popular series is about a boy named Henry and his dog, Mudge. Rylant published the first Henry and Mudge picture book in 1987. In 2006, *Henry and Mudge and the Great Grandpas* won the **Theodor Seuss Geisel Award**.

A Private Life

Rylant enjoys the freedom that being a writer gives her. She loves to go to the movies. She also takes walks with her dogs. Some afternoons, Rylant may do nothing but watch cartoons on television! Then, she may stay up all night writing a book.

Writing usually comes easily to Rylant. She says she often hears the story in her head. Other times, Rylant has to think a lot about what she's going to say. Sometimes she rearranges her furniture to help with the creative process!

Despite her success and awards, Rylant lives a very private life. She does not do book signings or tours. And, she rarely makes public appearances. Even her neighbors probably do not know what she does for a living.

Cynthia Rylant says writing has helped her feel better about herself. It also has helped her through some troubled times. "I hope one day to write a great book," she says. "A

magnificent book, which people will buy for those they love best. Which they will place in someone else's hands and say, 'Before you do anything else, you must read this.'" Rylant's fans might say this is a goal she has already reached.

Rylant illustrated her 1996 book **The Bookshop Dog.**

Glossary

autobiography - a story of a person's life that is written by himself or herself.

Caldecott Medal - an award the American Library Association gives to the artist who illustrated the year's best picture book. Runners-up are called Caldecott Honor Books.

controversial - of or relating to something that causes discussion between groups with strongly different views.

degree - a title given by a college to its graduates after they have completed their studies.

drum majorette - a girl or a woman who leads a marching band.

editor - a person who is in charge of preparing a work for publication.

graduate school - of, relating to, or engaged in studies beyond the first or bachelor's degree.

hepatitis - a disease of the liver.

Korean War - from 1950 to 1953. A war between North and South Korea. The U.S. government sent troops to help South Korea.

Newbery Medal - an award given by the American Library Association to the author of the year's best children's book. Runners-up are called Newbery Honor Books.

perspective - the position from which something is considered or looked at.

privy - a small building constructed over a pit that functions as an outdoor toilet.

pseudonym (SOO-duh-nihm) - a fictitious name, often used by an author.

Theodor Seuss Geisel Award - an award given by the American Library Association to the author and illustrator of the year's most distinguished American English-language book for beginning readers published in the United States. Runners-up are called Theodor Seuss Geisel Honor Books.

Web Sites

To learn more about Cynthia Rylant, visit ABDO Publishing Company on the World Wide Web at **www.abdopublishing.com**. Web sites about Cynthia Rylant are featured on our Book Links page. These links are routinely monitored and updated to provide the most current information available.

Index

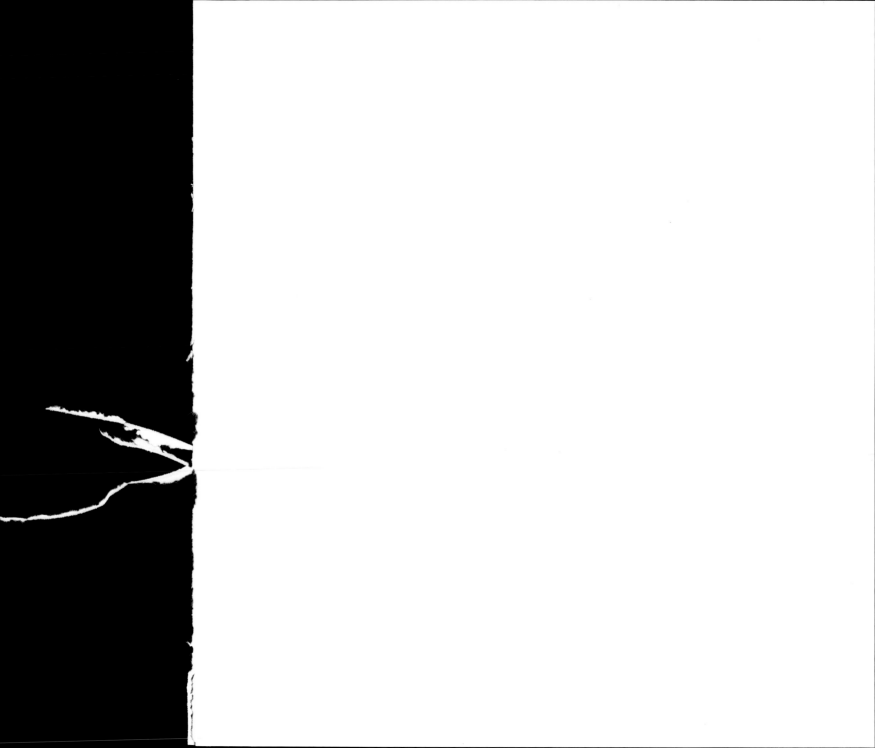